It's My State!

Utah

The Beehive State

Kerry Jones Waring, Doug Sanders, and Lisa M. Herrington

Cavendish
Square

New York

Published in 2016 by Cavendish Square Publishing, LLC
243 5th Avenue, Suite 136, New York, NY 10016

Copyright © 2016 by Cavendish Square Publishing, LLC

Third Edition

Website: cavendishsq.com

This publication represents the opinions and views of the author based on his or her personal experience, knowledge, and research. The information in this book serves as a general guide only. The author and publisher have used their best efforts in preparing this book and disclaim liability rising directly or indirectly from the use and application of this book.

CPSIA Compliance Information: Batch #CW16CSQ

All websites were available and accurate when this book was sent to press.

Library of Congress Cataloging-in-Publication Data

Sanders, Doug, 1972-
Utah / Doug Sanders, Lisa M. Herrington and Kerry Jones Waring.
pages cm. — (It's my state!)
Includes index.
ISBN 978-1-6271-3178-0 (hardcover) — ISBN 978-1-6271-3180-3 (ebook)
1. Utah—Juvenile literature. I. Herrington, Lisa M. II. Waring, Kerry Jones. III. Title.
F826.3.S36 2016
979.2—dc23

2015022186

Editorial Director: David McNamara
Editor: Fletcher Doyle
Copy Editor: Rebecca Rohan
Art Director: Jeffrey Talbot
Designer: Stephanie Flecha
Senior Production Manager: Jennifer Ryder-Talbot
Production Editor: Renni Johnson
Photo Research: J8 Media

Printed in the United States of America

UTAH
CONTENTS

A Quick Look at Utah 4

1. The Beehive State 7
Utah County Map 10
Utah Population by County 11
10 Key Sites 14
10 Key Plants and Animals 20

2. From the Beginning 23
The Native People 26
Making Sand Art 30
10 Key Cities 34
10 Key Dates in State History 43

3. The People 45
10 Key People 48
10 Key Events 54

4. How the Government Works 57
Political Figures from Utah 62
You Can Make a Difference 63

5. Making a Living 65
10 Key Industries 68
Recipe for Utah Scones 70

Utah State Map 74
Utah Map Skills 75
State Flag, Seal, and Song 76
Glossary 77
More About Utah 78
Index 79

State Tree: Quaking Aspen

The quaking aspen was selected as the state tree by the Utah legislature in 2014. This type of tree makes up about 10 percent of forest cover in the state. The quaking aspen is unique because a group of these trees develops a single root system to take nutrients from the soil.

State Bird: California Seagull

The California seagull is said to have saved Mormon pioneers' crops in 1848 by eating swarms of hungry crickets invading the fields. The event has come to be known as the Miracle of the Gulls. In honor of this bird, a statue called the Seagull Monument was erected in Salt Lake City, the state capital.

State Flower: Sego Lily

In 1911, Utah's schoolchildren chose the sego lily as the state flower. The graceful flower grows in the open rangeland of the state's Basin and Range region. The bulbs were eaten by the state's Native American population, as well as by Mormon settlers during their first grueling winter in the area.

★ State Animal: Rocky Mountain Elk

This hoofed mammal usually summers in the mountains and spends the winter grazing Utah's valleys. A member of the deer family, the Rocky Mountain elk was made the official state animal on February 1, 1971. The male Rocky Mountain elk has antlers that can span 5 feet (1.5 meters).

★ State Fossil: *Allosaurus*

Many *Allosaurus* fossils have been found in Utah. An average *Allosaurus* weighed 2 tons (1.8 metric tons) and was about 30 feet (9 m) long. These fearsome dinosaurs were among the most successful meat eaters of the late Jurassic period.

★ State Insect: Honeybee

Before it became nicknamed the Beehive State, Utah was once known as the Provisional State of **Deseret**. Deseret is a Mormon word that means "honeybee." This hardworking insect symbolized the perseverance of the early Mormon settlers. The honeybee officially became the state insect in 1983.

The snow-covered peaks of the Wasatch Range provide a majestic backdrop for Salt Lake City.

The Beehive State

For those who love the outdoors, Utah is a paradise. This western state is home to five national parks, seven national monuments, two national recreation areas, six national forests, and fourteen ski resorts. With a land area of 82,144 square miles (212,752 square kilometers), Utah ranks twelfth in size among the states. Although large, it would still take three Utahs to fit inside Texas. Utah is divided into twenty-nine counties.

In 1849, Utah's first white settlers—the Mormons—called their new state Deseret, a Mormon word for "honeybee." Bees represented the hard work of those early pioneers. Utah was later nicknamed the Beehive State. A beehive appears on the state flag and seal. It is also on the official state emblem.

Utah offers a full range of natural wonders to explore. Wind and water have carved amazing rock formations over millions of years. Looping arches and natural bridges are among the state's incredible sights.

Rock cliffs tower high above the flat deserts, which seem to be empty. But in the summer months, desert animals tend to be more active at sunset, finally free of the day's heat. As the sun dips into the west, the rock walls seem to glow in the red-orange light.

The Uinta Mountains in northeast Utah run east to west, unlike other ranges.

Snow-capped peaks of the Rocky Mountains jut straight into the sky. Utah inspires a sense of awe in visitors and residents alike. It is not surprising why. With its three main regions, Utah is truly a land of contrasts and dazzling beauty.

Rocky Mountains

The Rocky Mountains spread over a large part of western North America, extending from Canada in the north to Mexico in the south. The Uinta and Wasatch Mountain Ranges make up part of the Rocky Mountains in Utah.

The Uintas stretch across the northeastern corner of the state, running west from Colorado for about 150 miles (240 kilometers). They reach almost as far as Salt Lake City in north-central Utah. Named after the Ute tribe, the Uintas are a unique group of mountains. The Uintas are the only mountain range in North America that spread in an east to west direction. The spines of all the continent's other mountain chains line up north to south. But what makes the Uintas truly original is their striking beauty. Their rounded, snow-capped peaks are hard to miss in this part of the state.

Utah Borders	
North:	Idaho
	Wyoming
South:	Arizona
East:	Colorado
	Wyoming
West:	Nevada

The Wasatch Mountains start around Mount Nebo, near the center of the state, and extend north for about 250 miles (400 km) into parts of southeastern Idaho. They are popular with skiers, snowboarders, and mountain bikers. The eastern edge of the Wasatch starts as valleys and rolling plains. These slowly give way to high peaks and jagged irregular plateaus, or areas of raised land. During the last Ice Age, which ended about eleven thousand years ago, massive sheets of slow-moving ice called glaciers cut deep canyons in this rugged, ever-changing range. But perhaps its most striking feature is the steep western edge. There the mountains loom from 6,000 to 8,000 feet (1,828 to 2,438 m) above the valleys below. This sheer mountain wall is known as the Wasatch Front. Below this, the Basin and Range region begins.

Basin and Range Province

The Basin and Range Province, a large area that covers Nevada and extends south into Mexico, includes the western part of the state. This region makes up Utah's desert country. Spreading for miles, the sandy stretches of the Sevier and Escalante Deserts located here are among the driest places in the United States. These broad valleys, also known as basins, separate several impressive mountains that run north to south. Smaller mountain ranges mixed in with wide rounded basins are grouped in the center of the region. To

The Great Salt Lake is the saltiest lake in North America. The brine shrimp is one of the few aquatic animals that can live in it.

UTAH
COUNTY MAP

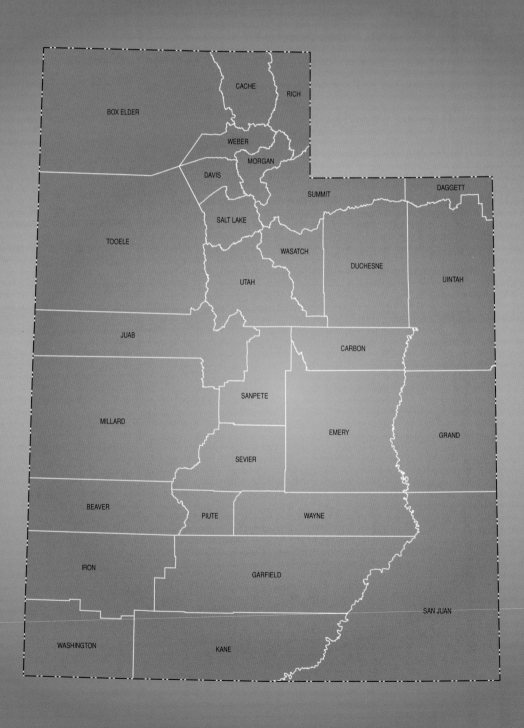

UTAH
POPULATION BY COUNTY

County	Population	County	Population	County	Population
Beaver County	6,629	Juab County	10,246	Tooele County	58,218
Box Elder County	49,975	Kane County	7,125	Uintah County	32,588
Cache County	112,656	Millard County	12,503	Utah County	516,564
Carbon County	21,403	Morgan County	9,469	Wasatch County	23,530
Daggett County	1,059	Piute County	1,556	Washington County	138,115
Davis County	306,479	Rich County	2,264	Wayne County	2,778
Duchesne County	18,607	Salt Lake County	1,029,655	Weber County	231,236
Emery County	10,976	San Juan County	14,746		
Garfield County	5,172	Sanpete County	27,822		
Grand County	9,225	Sevier County	20,802		
Iron County	46,163	Summit County	36,324		

Source: US Bureau of the Census, 2010

The part of Utah that intersects with three other states to form the Four Corners is in Washington County.

Cars have attempted to set records for fastest speed on land at the Bonneville Salt Flats for more than a century.

the east and west of the Basin and Range Province, the elevation starts to climb. Dusty plateaus give rise to larger mountain chains. They offer some of Utah's best soaring views.

In the northwestern part of the region lies the Great Salt Lake. This large body of water is about 75 miles (120 km) long and 35 miles (55 km) wide. The Great Salt Lake covers more than a million acres (405,000 hectares), or about 2,100 square miles (5,440 sq km). It is the largest natural lake west of the Mississippi River, and it is the largest saltwater lake in North America. It gets its name because the lake is saltier than the oceans. Dissolved minerals empty into the Great Salt Lake through four rivers and several streams. With no rivers or streams flowing out of the Great Salt Lake, large deposits of salt build up in the water. Companies now take salt from the lake and use it for a variety of purposes. The salt used on icy roadways, for instance, may come from the Great Salt Lake.

The Great Salt Lake is a remnant of a giant, ancient lake called Lake Bonneville. For thousands of years the water level rose and fell, until finally the lake dried up almost completely. What remained was a group of smaller lakes and a desert covered with salt and hard-caked soil. The Great Salt Lake Desert is famous for its salt beds. Today, the Bonneville Salt Flats cover parts of this desert. This vast stretch of smooth, white land is named after Lake Bonneville. It covers about 30,000 acres (12,140 ha).

Colorado Plateau

Utah's third natural region is the Colorado Plateau. This vast and varied region extends from the Uinta Basin to the high plateaus and deep canyons that mark southern Utah. The Uinta Basin is a bowl-shaped area located south of the Uinta Mountains. The Colorado Plateau covers more than half of the state—most of eastern and southern Utah. But the entire plateau stretches far beyond Utah's borders. It includes parts of Colorado, Arizona, and New Mexico.

The Colorado Plateau has a mix of features. High plateaus and mountains more than 11,000 feet (3,350 m) tall mark the western part of the region. These upland plains, as they are sometimes called, are not the flat and smooth places people usually think of as plains. Striped cliffs with pink, white, and red layers jut out of the land. Parts of the plateau are marked by curves folding into wondrous shapes. Ridges and mesas—flat-topped hills or mountains with steep sides—are bordered here and there by canyons, gorges, and valleys.

The Navajo consider the Rainbow Bridge to be a sacred site.

Antelope Island State Park

Arches National Park

Heber Valley Historic Railroad

1. Antelope Island State Park

The largest island on Great Salt Lake is 15 miles (24.2 km) long and about 5 miles (8 km) wide. It is home to more than forty freshwater springs and many forms of wildlife, including American bison.

2. Arches National Park

Called a "red rock wonderland," Arches National Park has more than two thousand natural stone arches. Landscape Arch has the longest span of any arch in North America. Park visitors can enjoy camping, biking, backpacking, or sightseeing.

3. Grand Staircase-Escalante National Monument

The Grand Staircase-Escalante National Monument covers more than 1.7 million acres (687,965 ha) of southern Utah. Geological features include canyons, plateaus, mesas, and buttes. In 2002, a seventy-five-million-year-old dinosaur skeleton was found here.

4. Heber Valley Historic Railroad

The Heber Valley Historic Railroad operates passenger trains between Heber City and Vivian Park, carrying an estimated ninety-four thousand passengers every year. The train passes several Utah landmarks on its route.

5. Hill Aerospace Museum

This museum is located within Hill Air Force Base near Ogden. Visitors can see more than ninety military aircraft, missiles, and aerospace vehicles. Hill Aerospace Museum is also home to the Utah Aviation Hall of Fame.

6. Lake Powell

Lake Powell is a reservoir on the Colorado River on the border between Utah and Arizona. Approximately two million people visit Lake Powell every year to enjoy boating, fishing, kayaking, and many other activities.

7. Loveland Living Planet Aquarium

This aquarium in Draper was started as a traveling exhibit in the van of a marine biologist, Brent Anderson, in 1999. The exhibit grew and the current museum was opened in 2014. About 2,400 animals are on display at the museum.

8. Temple Square

Temple Square in Salt Lake City is the location of many important facilities for the Church of Jesus Christ of Latter-day Saints. Visitors can see Salt Lake Temple, hear a performance by the Mormon Tabernacle Choir, or learn about the church's history.

9. Thanksgiving Point

Thanksgiving Point in Lehi is a farm, garden, and museum complex that offers educational, family-friendly activities. At the Museum of Ancient Life, you can see many dinosaur skeletons, fossils, and rocks.

10. Utah Olympic Park

Built for the 2002 Olympic Games in Park City, Utah Olympic Park is the place for trying a number of outdoor sports. Year-round activities include skiing, ziplining, and riding a bobsled on the official Olympic track.

Lake Powell

Temple Square

Utah Olympic Park

Zion, Bryce, and Cedar Breaks are some of the well-known canyons that add to the area's unique appearance. In the southeastern part of the state, the Colorado River is met by the Green River. These are the state's two main rivers. They have helped to carve out some of Utah's deepest canyons.

Rainbow Bridge is just one of the spectacular landforms located in the southern part of the state. It is the world's largest known bridge of natural rock, standing 278 feet (85 m) wide and 309 feet (94 m) high. Rainbow Bridge was formed when water eroded the sandstone. Nestled among the canyons, it is considered a sacred place by the Navajo tribe. The natural stone arch is accessible from Lake Powell, the second largest human-made lake in the world. The lake was created when Glen Canyon Dam was constructed on the Colorado River in Arizona. Construction of the dam was completed in 1963. It took fourteen years after its completion for the lake to fill.

Climate

After Nevada, Utah is the second-driest state in the country. Its deserts and lowlands receive little rainfall while other areas receive much more. For instance, the Great Salt Lake Desert receives less than 5 inches (13 centimeters) per year, while the mountains of the northeast average 50 inches (127 cm). The Wasatch Mountains

Powdery snow attracts skiers and snowboarders to Utah's many resorts.

often receive more than 60 inches (152 cm) of rain per year. Snow is common in the winter except along Utah's southern border and the Great Salt Lake Desert. In the north, it is an entirely different story. The ski areas near Salt Lake City have been known to receive more than 400 inches (1,000 cm) of snow each season. Some of the tallest mountain peaks even remain covered with snow throughout the summer.

Not surprisingly, in view of its varied landscapes, Utah has a climate of contrasts. Both the highest and the lowest temperatures ever recorded in the state happened in the same year. On February 1, 1985, the thermometers at Peter Sinks (a basin area in the Bear River Mountains) read 69 degrees below zero Fahrenheit (–56 degrees Celsius). Later that year, on July 5, the citizens of Saint George sizzled when the temperature reached 117°F (47°C)—but these are extremes. Mostly, the people of Utah enjoy weather that is somewhere in between. Average summer temperatures range from 60°F (15°C) in the northeast to 84°F (29°C) in the southwest. Winter temperatures average 20°F (–7°C) in the north and 39°F (4°C) in the south.

Plant Life

With such varied terrain, Utah is home to many types of trees and other plants. Some of these plants have special characteristics that enable them to thrive in the state's often harsh landscapes and high elevations. Juniper and sagebrush can be found in the Great Basin Desert. Wildflowers and meadow grasses thrive at higher elevations. In spring, flowering plants show their colors as they bloom throughout the state. Beavertail cacti distinguish themselves with showy red or purple petals. White sprays of dwarf bear claw poppies cling to rocks, and purple lupine sway in the breeze.

Forests blanket about 30 percent of the state, mostly near the mountains and on mountain slopes, where the soil is moist and fertile. Different types of trees are found at various elevations from the desert all the way to the tops of the mountains. In the desert, Joshua trees grow at low elevations. Douglas firs, piñon pines, willows, and quaking aspen grow in the mountains. On the relatively barren higher peaks, only the toughest trees survive. Bristlecone pines—some more than three thousand years old—manage to survive the strong winds and frigid cold temperatures year after year.

Prehistoric Discovery

A new species of dinosaur called *Lythronax argestes* was discovered at Utah's Grand Staircase-Escalante National Monument in 2009. The dinosaur was about 24 feet [7.3 m] long, had huge teeth, and is considered an ancestor of the famous *Tyrannosaurus rex*.

Animal Life

While perhaps appearing barren at first glance, Utah's deserts and other dry regions are actually home to several members of the animal kingdom. Poisonous scorpions live mostly under rocks. Scorpions and their ancestors have lived in Utah for more than four hundred million years. Reptiles such as rattlesnakes, lizards, and tortoises inhabit the state's dry regions. Desert horned lizards—sometimes called horned toads—live in the sandy areas of western Utah. Small mammals such as the desert shrew thrive in the dry and warm climate. Desert shrews are typically found in the southwestern part of the state.

Across Utah's grasslands, badgers shovel their way into the dirt, searching for a cool place to call home. With their strong legs, badgers can dig faster than humans. Coyotes can be found in the grasslands, forests, and other habitats. They typically travel alone, constantly on the lookout for jackrabbits and small rodents.

Utah's bodies of water are also home to a variety of wildlife. Fish such as trout, perch, carp, and bass live in the state's more than 11,000 miles (17,703 km) of streams and 147,000 acres (59,500 ha) of reservoirs and lakes. Frogs, salamanders, and other amphibians live in or near these bodies of water. Geese, mallard ducks, avocets, American white pelicans, and herons are some of the many birds that seek out the state's waters.

Birds soar through the skies above Utah. Golden eagles, hawks, sparrows, wrens, chickadees, ravens, woodpeckers, owls, and swallows are also among Utah's many feathered residents.

Utah's forests are filled with animals, including black bears, raccoons, bats, and squirrels. In the mountains, elk, mule deer, mountain goats, and pronghorns graze on grasses and other plants. Rocky Mountain bighorn sheep are a common sight along the mountain slopes.

Falcon Watch

Since 1984, peregrine falcons have been making nests and laying eggs in downtown Salt Lake City. Utah's Division of Wildlife Resources built a special nesting box on top of the Joseph Smith Memorial Building and set up cameras so residents can watch the baby birds hatch each spring.

For more than a hundred years, Antelope Island State Park has been home to herds of wild bison. The animals were brought to the island in 1893 in an attempt to save them from extinction. About six hundred of these animals now live on Antelope Island, the largest of the Great Salt Lake's ten islands. Deer, bobcats, coyotes, and several varieties of birds also inhabit the island.

Endangered Wildlife

Utah has several species of plants and animals that are considered endangered. An endangered species is at risk of becoming extinct or completely dying out. Human settlement, overhunting, pesticides, and pollution are some factors that threaten wildlife. Some of the state's endangered birds include the Mexican spotted owl and the whooping crane.

The number of Utah prairie dogs, who live nowhere else in the world, has decreased.

Another threatened species is the Utah prairie dog. It is one of several types of prairie dog in the state. These rodents make warning sounds that resemble a dog's bark. They can grow to be anywhere from 12 to 20 inches (30 to 50 cm) long, and they live together in underground burrows beneath grassy regions. During the day, these brown rodents come above ground to eat plants and insects. Gunnison's prairie dogs can be found in the southeast; white-tailed prairie dogs live in the northeast; and Utah prairie dogs live in the southwest.

Utah prairie dogs do not live in any other part of the world. Predators, disease, drought, and poisons have contributed to their decline in the past. Thanks to conservation efforts, however, their numbers are on the rebound. In September 2010, the US Fish and Wildlife Service announced a new plan that would continue to help Utah prairie dogs.

Beavertail Cacti

Desert Tortoise

Indian Paintbrush

1. Beavertail Cacti

Beavertail cacti can be found on the dry, rocky desert slopes of southwestern Utah. They get their name from their shape—flat and rounded, just like a beaver's tail. Bright red or lavender blooms sprout from this prickly plant from March through June.

2. Desert Bighorn Sheep

This sure-footed mammal is a master cliff-climber. Bighorn sheep usually live in groups, grazing on grasses and bushes during the day. They move to the valleys in autumn and return to the mountain pastures in the spring.

3. Desert Tortoise

Desert tortoises live off wildflowers and dried plants and grasses. Because of disease and habitat loss, the desert tortoise is a threatened species, which means they are at risk of becoming endangered in Utah.

4. Hopi Chipmunk

The Hopi chipmunk is a small rodent found in Utah, Colorado, and Arizona. It lives in rocky areas and feeds on seeds, flowers, other plants, and insects. They are most active in the early morning and late afternoon to avoid the midday sun.

5. Indian Paintbrush

This native plant sports a wide range of colors—yellow, red, orange, or cream. It grows best in sandy soils and usually blooms from March through May. Some types of Indian paintbrush tap into the roots of other plants and suck out nutrients.

UTAH ★ ★ ★ ★ ★ ★

6. Maguire Primrose

This flowering plant grows in the shade, in damp, moss-covered areas of Logan Canyon, in late April and May. Its flowers are rose or lavender, and it has broad spatula-shaped leaves. It is considered endangered.

7. Mojave Desert Sidewinder

This snake moves sideways by forming S-shaped curves with its body. It slides through the dry deserts, sand dunes, and rocky hillsides of Utah seeking lizards, kangaroo rats, and any other rodent that crosses its path.

8. Mule Deer

Mule deer get their name from their large, mule-like ears. The large ears flick about, trying to pick up the faint sound of approaching danger. These deer spend the warm months grazing in the mountains, but move to lower elevations in winter.

9. Navajo Sedge

Navajo sedge is an endangered plant species that grows in San Juan County. It has grass-like leaves and flowers that bloom in late June and July. The flowers are arranged in spikes. The plant has become endangered due to sheep grazing and groundwater pumping.

10. White River Beardtongue

This herb with a unique name is found in several locations across Utah, though the species is at risk of becoming endangered. Its lavender and pale blue flowers bloom from late May to June. It is a favorite food for sheep.

Mojave Desert Sidewinder

Mule Deer

White River Beardtongue

A Native American tribe called the Fremont created these petroglyphs at McKee Springs in Dinosaur National Monument.

From the Beginning

The first humans to live in what is now Utah are believed to have arrived about twelve thousand years ago. These early people were known as Paleo-Indians. Paleo means "older" or "ancient." Experts believe that they were descendants of people who came to North America using a natural land bridge that once connected Alaska and Asia. From there, these early people moved throughout North America.

The Paleo-Indians were nomadic. They traveled from place to place, hunting and gathering food. They lived off the region's abundant wildlife. Paleo-Indians used spears tipped with rock to hunt giant prehistoric animals, such as woolly mammoths.

A new group of ancient people—the Desert Archaic—inhabited the area about eight thousand years ago. At that time, people lived in simple settlements, either in small villages or in cave dwellings. Danger Cave and Jukebox Cave, both near Wendover, were both occupied at that time.

About twenty-five hundred years ago, agriculture became much more important to the inhabitants of the area. People planted corn, beans, and squash in the region's fertile valleys. In the Four Corners area—the only place in the United States where four states, including Utah, come together at one place—a people known today as the Ancestral Puebloans grew their own food and built their own cliff dwellings. These cliff dwellings,

Ancestral Puebloans built these cliff dwellings in Grand Gulch Primitive Area.

called pueblos, were made of adobe (mud) and built into canyon walls.

By 500 CE, a new group—the Fremont—had moved into the region. They were hunters and gatherers. They lived in pit houses—large hollows dug out of the ground. The Fremont left traces of their culture across Utah. Remains of their dwellings have been found throughout the state. Archaeologists have also discovered remnants of Fremont and Ancestral Puebloan tools, baskets, pottery, and clay figurines.

The Fremont also carved pictures on rock walls in the region. These rock carvings are called **petroglyphs**. They include animal shapes, as well as large human figures that have triangle-shaped shoulders and wear elaborate necklaces. Examples of these petroglyphs can be seen at the Fremont Indian State Park in Sevier. The park spans more than 1,000 acres (400 ha) and includes a visitor center, museum, and areas for camping, fishing, picnicking, and hiking.

Native Americans of the More Recent Past

After 1300 CE, other Native American groups sought out the area as well. The Ute, the Southern Paiute, the Navajo, the Goshute (or Gosiute), and the Northern and Eastern Shoshone all made the region their home. They hunted, fished, and gathered wild plants. The piñon nut, the fruit of a type of pine tree, became a popular treat. Groups of women, especially Paiute and Navajo, often trekked into the dry stretches of Utah countryside to gather the tiny nuts in baskets. Beginning in the 1600s, the Navajo in the Four Corners region herded sheep, goats, and cattle. They became known for their skill as weavers, making beautiful wool blankets with complex designs.

Utah's Native peoples lived in a variety of types of homes. Shelters made out of brush and cone-shaped tepees made from animal hides dotted the landscape. The Ute brought the tepee to Utah. It was a style they borrowed from the Native Americans who lived on the Great Plains. The Southern Paiute made rounded houses, called **wickiups**, which were formed by carefully arranging brush and poles. Some groups, such as the Goshute, moved from place to place, so they often searched for simple shelters. They gathered in caves or learned to make a short-term home out of the cracks and crevices in the landscape.

Although there were many different groups of people in the region, most Native Americans lived in peace. The Ute were known to be raiders and warriors, however. They searched out prosperous settlements and forced the people there to share their wealth. They also became skilled buffalo hunters, bearing down on these huge animals on their swift horses. The Ute and other groups began using horses after the Spanish brought the animals to the Americas in the 1500s. Horses changed life for Ute and other Native American groups. On horseback, Native Americans could more easily hunt large game, attack neighboring villages, or travel great distances.

Explorers, Trappers, and Traders

During the mid-1700s, Spanish explorers from Mexico traveled through what is now Utah. Juan Maria de Rivera was the first Spanish explorer known to visit the region. Starting in 1765, he led at least two expeditions into what is now Utah. De Rivera and his group reached the Colorado River near present-day Moab in the southeastern part of the state.

More than a decade later, another chapter in European exploration was added. Two Franciscan priests, Francisco Atanasio Domínguez and Silvestre Vélez de Escalante, led a team

This painting depicts trappers moving pelts by boat on the Bear River.

The Native People

People have been living in the region now known as Utah for more than twelve thousand years. The earliest people in this area were known as Paleo-Indians. They hunted wooly mammoths and bison. About 2,500 years ago, groups now known as the Fremont and Ancestral Pueblo, or Anasazi, lived there. They grew simple crops and created art such as baskets and clay figures. The ancestors of modern tribes lived in Utah starting about nine hundred years ago. In the modern area, Utah was home to five key Native American tribes leading up to and including the time of European settlement. These tribes were known as the Ute, Paiute, Goshute, Shoshone, and Navajo.

The Ute, Paiute, Goshute, and Shoshone speak languages that share a common root. Their language family is known as the Numic language family. These groups also had many aspects of their lifestyle and culture in common. They lived in small, family-centered groups and moved around a lot to find food by hunting and gathering. Roots, plants, and nuts were key parts of their diets, as well as fish and small animals. Piñon nuts were a common food for Utah's Native Americans. Many lived in tepees though others lived in wickiups.

The arrival of European settlers changed the way of life of Utah's Native people. Many Navajo were killed or enslaved when Spanish settlers arrived in the seventeenth century.

Many Native American tribes, including the Paiute, lived in wickiups. This one was photographed early in the twentieth century.

Some Navajo joined with the Pueblo people to rebel against the Spanish, and as a result, many Navajo and Pueblo intermarried and began to share some of their culture. In 1863, Kit Carson, appointed by the US government, drove many Native Americans from their land and forced them to walk 300 miles (483 km) in an event now known as the Long Walk. The settlement of Mormon people further displaced many of Utah's Native Americans. Thousands moved to reservations or neighboring states.

Today, the eight federally recognized tribes in Utah include the Navajo Nation and several small tribes or bands of Paiute, Ute, Goshute, and Shoshone. There are five groups in the Paiute Indian Tribe of Utah.

Spotlight on the Paiute People

In addition to Utah, the Paiute people have lived in California, Arizona, and Nevada. Traditionally, the Paiute lived in family-based groups and traveled frequently to find food.

Distribution: Today, the Paiute live mostly on reservations covering about 4,000 acres (1,619 ha) in southwestern Utah. This land is located near the cities of Ivins and Cedar City.

Food: Plants were an important part of the traditional Paiute diet. They were known to use as many as ninety-six different kinds of plants. They farmed corn, squash, and beans and gathered wild plants, roots, and nuts. The Paiute also hunted fish, birds, and many kinds of mammals.

Homes: Most Paiute lived in wickiups, small cone-shaped shelters covered in brush. Some also lived in tepees.

Traditions: The Paiute people prayed to the spirits of nature to show respect and gratitude to them. They called their most powerful spirit "the one who made the earth." They believed these spirits existed in parts of the natural world, such as the sun, the coyote, and the wolf.

Government: Traditionally, the Paiute lived in small groups made up of about three to five households or families. Sometimes these smaller groups were part of larger groups. They held council meetings to make decisions together. While each community had a leader, called a *niave*, he did not tell the members of the tribe what to do. Instead, he worked with them to provide guidance and help carry out the decisions made by the group.

that left Santa Fe in present-day New Mexico. They hoped to spread Christianity among the Native Americans of the region. These explorers also wanted to find an overland route between Santa Fe and California. They entered Utah from the east and trekked through the Uinta Basin, crossing the Wasatch Mountains. They ended up at tribal camps along what is now called Utah Lake, the state's largest freshwater lake. Turning south, they followed the edge of the mountain chain, crossing the Colorado River. But their hopes of reaching Monterey, California, were dashed by fierce blizzards. The group returned to Santa Fe in 1777.

Those first steps eventually led to the well-worn paths of settlement. However, people of European descent did not begin settling in the region until the next century. By the early 1800s, trade routes had been set up between Santa Fe and the Native Americans of north-central Utah. Fur trappers and traders called "mountain men" crisscrossed the region. Spain claimed the region, and then Mexico, after Mexico won its independence from Spain in 1821. People came from all directions, however, including Americans from the east and Canadians from the north. Americans probably first came to the region in 1811 or 1812. Most came in search of the valuable furs of beavers and other fur-bearing animals.

By the 1820s, most of Utah had been explored and mapped. One of the most legendary trappers, Jim Bridger, first spotted the Great Salt Lake in 1824. When he tasted its saltiness, he thought it was an ocean. Bridger was one of the mountain men recruited by William H. Ashley, who hired trappers to work for his fur-trading company, which was based in St. Louis, Missouri. Each spring, Ashley collected furs from the trappers at a meeting spot along the Green River in Utah.

French-Canadian Étienne Provost was a successful fur trapper and trader who earned the nickname "the Man of the Mountains." Several places in central Utah are named after him, including the Provo River, Provo Canyon, and the city of Provo.

In Their Own Words

"The object of our anxious search, the waters of the inland sea, stretching in still and solitary grandeur far beyond the limits of our vision."
—John C. Frémont, upon seeing Great Salt Lake for the first time in 1843

In the 1840s, an official US government scouting party bound for California passed through Utah. Army engineer John C. Frémont, known as the Pathfinder of the West, mapped countless trails through the land that is now Utah. Fur trapper and

Fur trapper Étienne Provost was known as "the Man of the Mountains."

frontiersman Kit Carson joined him as a guide on later expeditions. Through written records, Frémont added to the growing knowledge of the area's plant and animal life. A mapmaker, Charles Preuss, worked with Frémont to create detailed and reliable maps of the areas he explored. Frémont's wife, Jessie, helped him write lively, colorful descriptions of his travels with the goal of encouraging people to travel west and settle there. His maps helped later pioneers find the fastest and safest routes through Utah.

Mormon Country

For the area's Native Americans, after centuries of living in a world without borders, life was about to change. A wave of white settlers eager to head west in search of religious freedom soon poured into the region. This first group to create permanent settlements in Utah was the Mormons.

Mormons belong to the Church of Jesus Christ of Latter-day Saints. Joseph Smith Jr. founded this church in Western New York in 1830. Smith and his followers believed that Christ had returned to Earth to preach among the people. Their beliefs were laid out in the *Book of Mormon*. But Smith's teachings were unpopular with many people. The Mormons faced violence and mistrust nearly everywhere they went. They were often forced to move from town to town. In June 1844, Smith was killed in jail in Carthage, Illinois, by an angry mob that disagreed with Mormon beliefs.

Leadership of the Mormon church then fell to Brigham Young. He decided to lead his people west in search of a new homeland. Their long, hard journey from Nauvoo, Illinois, by wagon trains began on February 4, 1846. The first group made its way to Nebraska and set up a camp called Winter Quarters, near present-day Omaha, to wait for spring. From Winter Quarters, on April 16, 1847, a scouting party of 148 pioneers set off in search of a new place to settle. The small group included 143 men (three of whom were African American), three women, and two children.

Frémont's maps and reports helped convince the Mormon pioneers that what is now Utah was the place where they would finally find a permanent home. Some of the group entered the Salt Lake Valley on July 22, 1847. Another part of the group, including Young, arrived two days later.

Making Sand Art

Utah is known for its stunning, rocky landscapes, including the layered **sedimentary rocks** of the Grand Staircase and many other formations. Make your own sand art to recreate the look of these natural wonders. Sand art makes a great gift for your friends, family, or teachers, too!

What You Need

2 cups (473 milliliters) of sand or fine table salt
(Ask an adult before using salt from the kitchen)
Colored chalk

Small jars or bottles
A tray or paper plates
Spoons or a small scoop

What To Do

- Place a small amount of sand on the paper plate or tray. Pick a chalk color that you wish to be your first sand layer.
- Rub the chalk over the sand. The sand will start to pick up the color. Continue to do so until it is the shade you want. You can also use a spoon or butter knife to "shave" the chalk onto the sand and mix it together.
- Use your spoon to scoop the colored sand into the jar.
- Repeat with as many colors as you wish to include in your art.
- Carefully add each color of sand layer by layer to the jar.
- Seal the jar with a lid or plastic wrap when complete.
- You can decorate the jar with ribbon or stickers for an extra touch.
- Store leftover sand in a tightly sealed plastic bag or container to use later.

Brigham Young reached the Great Salt Lake in 1847 and helped the Mormons build a settlement where they could practice their religion.

Many others would later join them. A large number of Mormon pioneers made their journey in covered wagons. From 1856 to 1860, others traveled on foot, pushing their household items in handcarts. This period became known as the Handcart Migration. Because many of these pioneers were traveling from the Midwest, they attempted to travel during the spring and summer months in order to avoid dangerous winter weather. Two groups of settlers known as the Willie Company and the Martin Company were not as fortunate. They departed for Utah in the summer of 1856. The journey became complicated and dangerous through the autumn and into the winter months, and by the time those groups reached Utah in November, many of them had died, and those who remained had lost many possessions.

The settlers immediately got to work building their new society. The pioneers constructed irrigation systems across the desert so they could water crops. In 1848, the settlers faced the challenge of a drought, frost, and a plague of crickets threatening their harvest. Flocks of seagulls ate many of the crickets, and the Mormon settlers were able to

The Journey's End monument in This is the Place Heritage Park honors Utah's earliest settlers.

save enough crops to make it through that winter. The seagull was later named the state bird of Utah out of gratitude.

In the first few years, life was hard for the Mormons. But this was not the first challenge they had faced. They were armed with determination, a strong group ethic, and of course, their faith. By 1869, about seventy thousand Mormon pioneers had trekked across the plains and settled in Utah.

Young planned for a beautiful city to be built at the northern end of the Salt Lake Valley. It was called Great Salt Lake City. In 1868, "Great" was dropped from the name. The Mormon church's ruling body served as the region's first government. Starting out as a small frontier outpost, Salt Lake City grew into Utah's major urban center.

Salt Lake City serves as the state capital today, and it is home to many historic sites. Young designated the site where Salt Lake Temple would be built. The temple was constructed out of Utah granite as the centerpiece of the city's Temple Square. It took forty years to build. Only Mormons can enter Salt Lake Temple. Nearby is the dome-shaped Mormon Tabernacle where the famous Mormon Tabernacle Choir sings. It is known for its huge pipe organ. Also in the area is Young's family home, called the Beehive House.